Math on Halloween

The Properties of Multiplication and Division

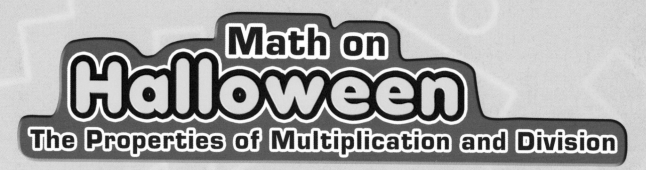

Ian F. Mahaney

PowerKiDS press

New York

Published in 2013 by The Rosen Publishing Group, Inc.
29 East 21st Street, New York, NY 10010

First Edition

Editor: Joanne Randolph
Book Design: Greg Tucker

Photo Credits: Cover © www.iStockphoto.com/Maria Pavlova; p. 4 Sean Locke/The Image Bank/ Getty Images; p. 5 K Welschmeyer/Shutterstock.com; p. 6 © www.iStockphoto.com/Yvan Dubé; p. 7 © www.iStockphoto.com/Viorika Prikhodko; p. 8 Margaret I. Wallace/Shutterstock.com; pp. 9 (left), 15 Greg Tucker; p. 9 (right) Comstock Images/Getty Images; pp. 10–11 iStockphoto/Thinkstock; p. 12 © www.iStockphoto.com/Valerie Loiseleux; p. 13 Jupiterimages/Comstock Images/Getty Images; p. 14 Jupiterimages/FoodPix/Getty Images; pp. 16–17, 18–19 Sean Locke/The Agency Collection/Getty Images; pp. 20–21 Image Source/Getty Images.

Library of Congress Cataloging-in-Publication Data

Mahaney, Ian F.
 Math on Halloween : the properties of multiplication and division / by Ian F. Mahaney. — 1st ed.
   p. cm. — (Core math skills)
 Includes index.
 ISBN 978-1-4488-9654-7 (library binding) — ISBN 978-1-4488-9766-7 (pbk.) — ISBN 978-1-4488-9767-4 (6-pack)
 1. Multiplication—Juvenile literature. 2. Division—Juvenile literature. 3. Halloween—Juvenile literature. I. Title.
 QA115.M228 2013
 513.2'13—dc23
                                   2012023590

Manufactured in the United States of America

CPSIA Compliance Information: Batch #W13PK4: For Further Information contact Rosen Publishing, New York, New York at 1-800-237-9932

Contents

Trick-or-Treat Math

Trick-or-treating on Halloween is a lot of fun. It may not seem like it has much to do with math. We can count, add, subtract, and more using our candy, though. The following pages will take a look at how Halloween can teach us about the **properties** of multiplication and division.

If four trick-or-treaters each take three pieces of candy, how many pieces do they take in all? The math sentence would be 4 x 3 = 12.

Think about this problem. If your uncle buys three pumpkins each for seven kids, the math sentence would look like this: 3 pumpkins x 7 kids = 21 pumpkins. If your uncle buys 7 pumpkins each for 3 kids, he also buys a total of 21 pumpkins: 3 kids x 7 pumpkins = 21 pumpkins. This means 7 x 3 = 3 x 7 = 21. Changing the order of the **factors** multiplied does not change the **product**. This is the **commutative property** of multiplication.

Figure It Out

A family has two pumpkins. After Halloween, they decide to bake pumpkin pies. If each pumpkin makes five pies, how many pies can they make?

(See answers on p. 22)

Costumes by the Yard

Wearing costumes when trick-or-treating is fun. Some people like to buy costumes. Others like to make them. Either way, your math **skills** will help you.

If you decide to make a costume, multiplication can help you figure out how much **fabric** to buy. Let's say you are making a bat costume. To make the wings, you need a piece of fabric that is 9 feet (3 m) long. If there are three

people making bat costumes and they each need 9 feet of fabric for the wings, together they need 9 x 3 = 27 feet of fabric. Fabric is generally measured in yards, and 1 yard equals 3 feet. This means that 27 feet ÷ 3 = 9 yards. Did you notice that 9 x 3 = 27 and 27 ÷ 3 = 9? If you divided 27 by 9, do you know what the answer would be? It would be 27 ÷ 9 = 3.

For some costumes, you may need to buy makeup. If you have to buy three packages of different makeup that all cost $15, the multiplication sentence to find out how much that would cost would be: 3 x 15 = 45.

Four siblings go to a costume shop with three $20 bills. How much can each one spend on a costume?

Figure It Out

(See answers on p. 22)

Halloween Party

Halloween parties are a time to play spooky games and eat treats. A party takes planning, though, and you can use math to help you!

Let's say you want to make a Halloween cake decorated with a spider-web design. You want to be sure

If 6 cupcakes fit on each serving plate and you have 30 cupcakes, how many plates would you need? The math sentence that helps you is 30 ÷ 6 = 5.

all your guests can have a piece of cake. If your cake has eight slices and there are 24 guests coming to the party, you would write the math sentence like this: $24 \div 8 = 3$.

This diagram shows how 8 slices x 3 cakes = 24 slices.

You want to play the game in which you try to eat doughnuts without your hands at your party. You need to figure out how many doughnuts to buy. If you are planning to let 15 guests each try two times, you need at least 15 x 2 = 30 doughnuts.

Figure It Out

There is a Halloween party with 10 people attending. The host makes five bat-shaped cookies for each guest. How many cookies does the host need to make? Does the number of cookies change if the host invites five people and makes 10 cookies for each of them?

(See answers on p. 22)

Trick or Treat!

A group of five kids collects candy from nine houses on a block. Every house gives each child two pieces of candy. We can figure out how many pieces of candy the kids will have at the end. We know 5 kids x 2 pieces of candy = 10 pieces of candy at one house. In the end, they will have 10 x 9 = 90 pieces of candy.

The **associative property** of multiplication says that when multiplying three or more numbers, any two numbers can be multiplied first and still give the same result. We can write (2 x 5) x 9 = 10 x 9 = 90 and 2 x (5 x 9) = 2 x 45 = 90. No matter how you write it, that's a lot of candy!

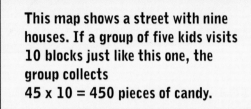

This map shows a street with nine houses. If a group of five kids visits 10 blocks just like this one, the group collects
45 x 10 = 450 pieces of candy.

If five kids trick-or-treat on one block that has 12 houses and each house has two families, how many pieces of candy will the group collect? Each family gives each child one piece of candy.

(See answers on p. 22)

Figure It Out

How Many Pieces?

Some houses give out more than one piece of candy. A group of 20 kids visits a house whose owner gives each kid three pieces of candy. To find the total number of pieces of candy the group got, we write: 20 x 3 = 60 pieces of candy.

This picture shows how multiplication relates to addition.

20   +   20   +   20   =   20 x 3 = 60

The owner buys candy in bags that hold 20 pieces of candy. To find out how many bags of candy he would need for this group, the math sentence would be: $60 \div 20 = 3$ bags of candy.

Do you see how multiplication and division are **inverses**? Their operations undo one another. We began with 3. We multiplied 3 by 20 to get 60. Then we divided 60 by 20 to get 3.

Figure It Out

If a group of seven kids collects 12 pieces of candy each, how many pieces do they have in total? What happens when you divide that total by the number of kids?

(See answers on p. 22)

Sorting the Loot

There are many types of candy given out on Halloween. There is chocolate, licorice, chewy candies, and many others. After trick-or-treating, you may want to sort your candy.

If you have 80 pieces of candy, there are many ways you can sort the candy. There are many ways you

can use math to talk about, or **express**, how much of each kind you have, too. If you have 40 chocolate bars and you want to find out what fraction of your candy that is, you can express it like this:

$\frac{1}{2} = \frac{40}{80}$ or $40 \div 80 = 0.5$ is the amount of your candy that is chocolate. What if you have 20 chewy candies and want to find the percentage of your candy that is chewy? You can multiply the fraction $\frac{20}{80}$ by 100:

$(\frac{1}{4}) \times 100 = (\frac{20}{80}) \times 100 = .25 \times 100 = 25\%$.

25% chewy candy	25% gum
50% chocolate	

If you use multiplication to help find out what percentage of each kind of candy you have in your basket, you can show what you have found in a pie chart like this one.

You have 10 chocolate bars, 10 pieces of licorice, and 10 gummy candies. You give the 10 gummy candies to your friend. Of your remaining candies, what percentage is chocolate?

Figure It Out

(See answers on p. 22)

Dividing It Up

After trick-or-treating, you decide to share your candy. Say you want to split your loot into thirds. You will keep $\frac{1}{3}$, share $\frac{1}{3}$, and donate $\frac{1}{3}$ to kids who cannot trick-or-treat.

If you collected 90 pieces of candy, you will need to figure out how much $\frac{1}{3}$ of 90 equals. There are two ways to do this. One is by dividing and the other is by multiplying. You can divide 90 by 3: $90 \div 3 = 30$. You can also multiply 90 by $\frac{1}{3}$: $90 \times (\frac{1}{3}) = 30$. Do you see how **similar** multiplication and division are?

You and a friend each collected 65 pieces of Halloween candy. If each of you donates half of your Halloween candy to children in the hospital, how many pieces will you have donated?

(See answers on p. 22)

Figure It Out

Going, Going, Gone . . .

The **distributive property** of multiplication helps you simplify multiplication problems. The rule says that you can break up numbers by adding them. Let's look at a Halloween example.

Two brothers eat 12 pieces of candy total in a day. How many do they eat in a week? The multiplication problem can be written as 12 pieces x 7 days. Fred eats 8 pieces a day and Bill eats 4. The distributive property allows you to multiply the smaller numbers then add them together:

12 x 7 = (8 + 4) x 7 = (8 x 7) + (4 x 7) = 56 + 28 = 84. When you know how to multiply small numbers, you can use the distributive property to multiply larger numbers.

Let's say you and your friend each have 5 chewy candies and 10 chocolate bars. We can use the distributive property to find out how much candy you have in all. Using the distributive property looks like this:
$2 \times (5 + 10) = (2 \times 5) + (2 \times 10) = 10 + 20 = 30$.

If admission to a haunted house costs $4, how much will it cost a school of 120 people to get in? The distributive property can help you find the answer.

Figure It Out

(See answers on p. 22)

Halloween Math

There is a lot of math that has to do with Halloween. You have reviewed the commutative property, the associative property, and the distributive property.

You have also reviewed how closely multiplication and division are linked. Halloween reminds us that division is multiplication's inverse. You have 24 Halloween cookies. If you multiply 24 by any number then divide that product by the same number, you will get 24. Try it on a piece of scrap paper. For example, $8 \times 24 = 192$ and $192 \div 8 = 24$. Can you think of other Halloween treats and tricks you can multiply and divide?

Bobbing for apples is a fun game to play at Halloween parties. If there are six adults at a party and seven kids, how many apples are needed if everybody gets two apples?

(See answers on p. 22)

Figure It Out: The Answers

Page 5: **They will be able to make 5 x 2 = 10 pies.**

Page 7: **The siblings have $20 x 3 = $60. There are four of them, so each one can spend $60 ÷ 4 = $15.**

Page 9: **The host needs to make 10 x 5 = 50 cookies. The answer does not change when the number of guests and cookies are switched, because of the commutative property.**

Page 11: **The group will collect (2 x 12) x 5 = 24 x 5 = 120 pieces of candy. The associative property says we can express this as 2 x (12 x 5) = 2 x 60 = 120 pieces of candy.**

Page 13: **In total, the kids collect 7 x 12 = 84 pieces of candy. Dividing the amount of candy by the number of children gives us: 84 ÷ 7 = 12.**

Page 15: **You have 10 + 10 + 10 = 30 pieces of candy. You give away 10 gummies, leaving you with 30 – 10 = 20 pieces of candy. Of those pieces, 10 are chocolate so the percentage that is chocolate is $(\frac{10}{20})$ x 100 = $(\frac{1}{2})$ x 100 = 50%.**

Page 17: **Combined, you and your friend have 65 x 2 = 130 pieces of candy. Find half by dividing that total by 2: 130 ÷ 2 = 65.**

Page 19: **To get into the haunted house, it will cost them 120 x $4 = (100 + 20) x $4 = (100 x $4) + (20 x $4) = $400 + $80 = $480**

Page 21: **There are 6 + 7 = 13 people at the party so the party needs 13 x 2 = 26 apples.**

Glossary

associative property (uh-SOH-shee-ay-tiv PRO-pur-tee)
A rule in multiplication that says that when three or more numbers are multiplied together, any two can be multiplied first and still find the same result.

commutative property (kuh-MYOO-tuh-tiv PRO-pur-tee)
A rule in multiplication that says the order in which numbers are multiplied does not change the result.

distributive property (dih-STRIH-byoo-tiv PRO-pur-tee)
A rule in multiplication that allows bigger numbers to be split into smaller numbers.

express (ik-SPRES) To say mathematically.

fabric (FA-brik) Cloth.

factors (FAK-turz) Numbers that are multiplied together.

inverses (in-VERS-ez) Opposites that undo one another.

product (PRAH-dukt) The result of a multiplication problem.

properties (PRAH-pur-teez) Features that belong to something.

similar (SIH-muh-ler) Almost the same as.

skills (SKILZ) Abilities or things that help one do a job well.

Index

Websites

Due to the changing nature of Internet links, PowerKids Press has developed an online list of websites related to the subject of this book. This site is updated regularly. Please use this link to access the list:
www.powerkidslinks.com/cms/hall/

24